The people of the world made God sad because they did bad things and hurt each other.

God told Noah; "I will send water to cover the whole earth, but I will save your loving family and the animals."

"I want you to build a big boat;" God continued.
"We'll call it an Ark! Here are all the instructions."

Many people laughed at Noah. "You are crazy!" they said. "It's never even rained before. Ha! Ha! Ha! Ho! Ho! Ho!"

But Noah didn't stop just because people made fun of him. He kept on working and building the boat. What a big job!

When Noah finally finished building the big Ark, God sent two of each kind of animal.

They all went into the boat. There were big animals and little ones, fast animals and slow ones too.

All the animals had a place on the Ark, a cozy little corner to get comfortable in. After all, it was going to be a loooong ride.

**Then God closed the door with a big WHAM!
Noah's family and the animals were now safe and sound inside.**

Rain fell, lightning flashed, and thunder rumbled! What a noise!

**More and more rain fell until water covered the ground.
The Ark began to float higher and higher.**

**It rained for so many many days.
The boat rocked and splashed around.**

The animals inside felt like thy were on a roller-coaster ride, while the fish outside had more water than ever to swim in.

Noah, his wife, their sons and their wives, were kept quite busy feeding all the animals in the Ark.

It wasn't always pleasant or easy, and it smelled like a zoo.
But Noah and his family trusted God.

**They prayed and waited, prayed and waited.
And one day the rain stopped and the sun shone!**

"Now we just have to wait for the water to dry up!" said Noah.

Some time later, Noah sent a bird, to fly up high and down low, and to check out the situation of the ground.

**It finally came back with a branch.
"That means dry land is nearby!" said Noah joyfully.**

The exciting day arrived; when Noah's family and all the animals could finally come out of the Ark!

**They breathed fresh air and stepped on the ground!
It felt wonderful not to be rocking on a boat any more.**

Noah praised God for His greatness and for keeping them safe!

God put the very first rainbow in the sky. "Now every time you see one, remember My love and power!" God said.

**Noah continued to love and trust God thoughout the rest of his life.
What a great lesson we can learn from him.**

iCHARACTER

Published by iCharacter Ltd. (Ireland)
www.icharacter.org
By Agnes and Salem de Bezenac
Illustrated by Agnes de Bezenac
Copyright 2015. All rights reserved.

Copyright © 2015 by iCharacter Ltd. All rights reserved. No part of this book may be reproduced in any form or by any electronic or mechanical means, including information storage and retrieval systems, without written permission from the publisher or author, except in the case of a reviewer, who may quote brief passages embodied in critical articles or in a review.

Printed by BoD in Norderstedt, Germany